*Commissioned by the American Guild of Organists*
*For the 2001 Regional Competitions for Young Organists (RCYO)*

*Dedicated to my mother, Hester H. Locklair, on a significant birthday, 1998*

# Jubilo
## (A Prelude for Organ)

by

# Dan Locklair

ISBN 0-634-01893-0

**RICORDI**

DISTRIBUTED BY

7777 W. BLUEMOUND RD. P.O. BOX 13819 MILWAUKEE, WI 53213

# Jubilo
## (A Prelude for Organ)

**Jubilo (A Prelude for Organ)** is the result of a 1998 autumn commission from the American Guild of Organists (AGO) for the 2001 Regional Competitions for Young Organists (RCYO). The commission is the first by the RCYO, an AGO-sponsored competition for organists aged 22 and under, and I wish to thank the RCYO Committee for awarding it to me. Performance of **Jubilo** will be required of all competitors entering the 2001 Competitions. **Jubilo** is dedicated to my mother, Hester H. Locklair, a church school teacher of the young for many years, in celebration of her significant 1998 birthday.

Approximately six minutes in length, **Jubilo** is a single-movement composition in four primary sections. The opening section, marked "Expansive and expressive," has the two hands alternating between a broad, ever-shifting melodic line (where the same pitches are recycled on each restatement, but with a new melodic contour) and four chordal sonorities that, with the pedal, form a short chaconne. The four pedal pitches (D, E, G, A) represent the primary musical material on which the entire piece is built. Following the climax of the first section, a trill in the manuals propels the piece forward into **Jubilo's** fast and rhythmic middle section. Marked "Quick and vibrant," dialogues between the manuals abound, soon leading to the entrance of the pedal's joyous melodic idea. The presence of both ideas, in repetition and in development continues, and their alternation forms the core of this section. After building to a dramatic climax over a pedal trill, a variant of the piece's opening section, marked "Expansive, with sweep" and underpinned by double pedaling, returns. Soon a brief variant of the fast section, marked "Quick and vibrant," emerges to conclude **Jubilo** with the power of full organ, resoundingly expressing the extra-musical stimulus for this piece as found in the Latin word "jubilo"–"to let out whoops of joy."

Dan Locklair
Winston-Salem, NC/USA
December 1998

Duration : ca. 6 minutes

### Performance Note

**Jubilo** may be effectively played on an organ of two manuals and pedal. Very little change in registration is required. Though registration suggestions are given for a two manual organ, if a larger instrument is available, the performer is free to expand, musically and with good taste, the registration suggestions.

D.L.

*Commissioned by the American Guild of Organists*
*For the 2001 Regional Competitions for Young Organists (RYCO)*

*Commissioned by the American Guild of Organists*
*for the 2001 Regional Competitions for Young Organists (RCYO)*

*Dedicated to my mother, Hester H. Locklair, on a significant birthday, 1998*

# Jubilo
## (A Prelude for Organ)

Sw. Foundations 8', 4', 2', Mixture(s)
Gt. Foundations 8', 4', 2', Mixture(s), Trumpet 8'
   (Sw. to Gt. 8')
Pd. Foundations 16', 8', 4', Sw. to Pd. 8'

Dan Locklair

**Expansive and expressive**  ( 𝅗𝅥 = ca. 40)

© Copyright 2000 by CASA RICORDI, a division of BMG Music Publishing Canada Inc.
International Copyright Secured
Hal Leonard Corporation - Sole Sales Agent

**Quick and vibrant**  ( ♩ = ca. 152)

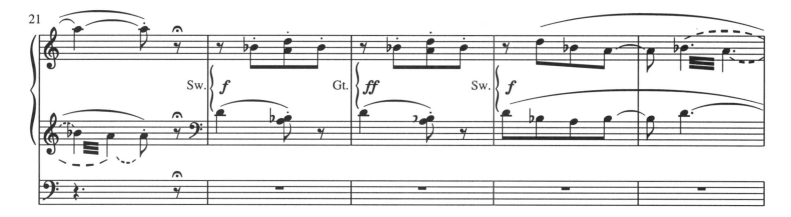

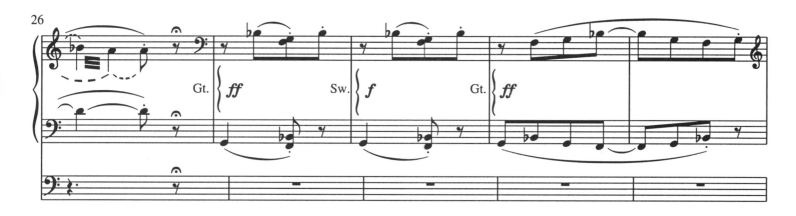

* The adding and omitting of Gt. to Pd. 8' throughout is optional, for the pedal may be effectively and tastefully
registered to balance with both manuals. Care should be taken not to overwhelm completely the softer manual.

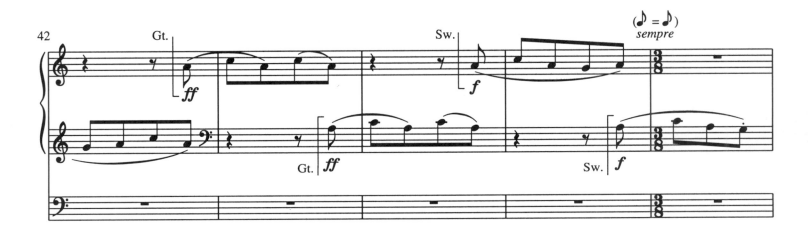

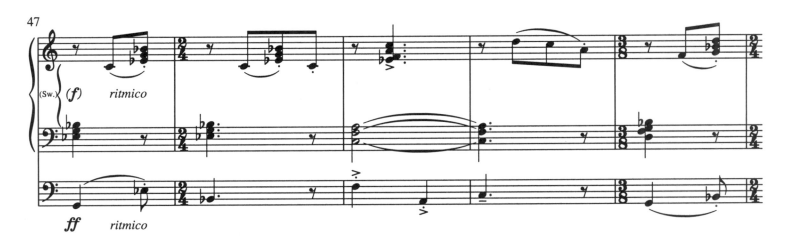

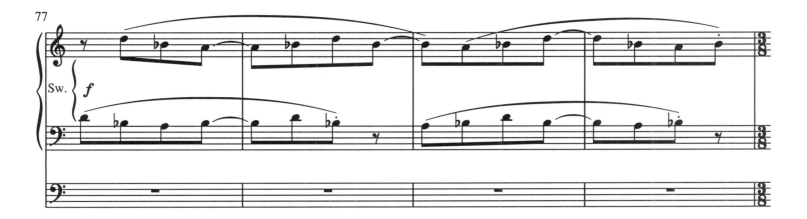

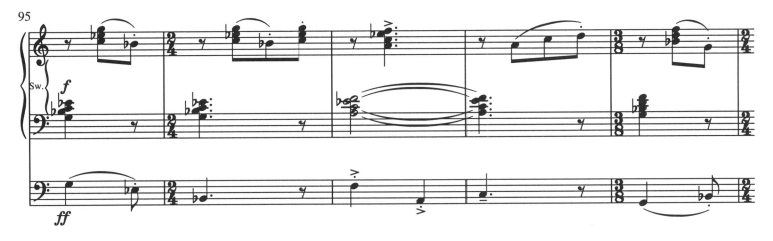

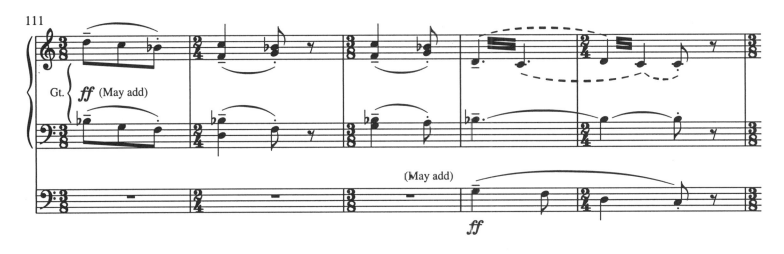

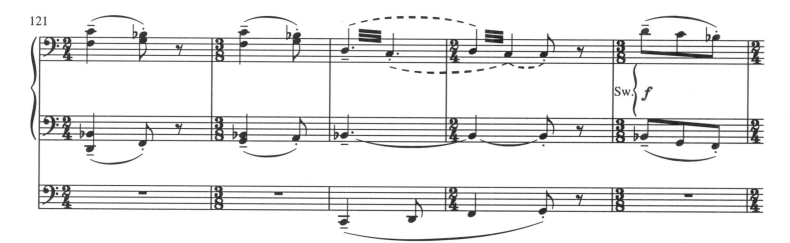

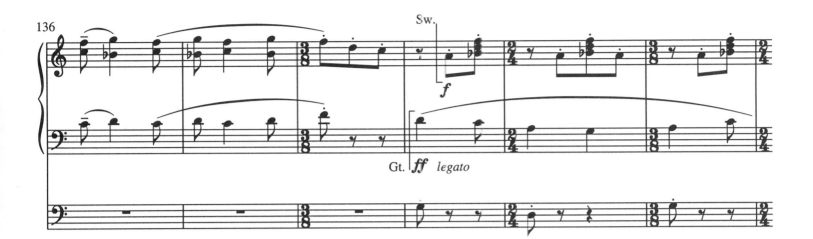

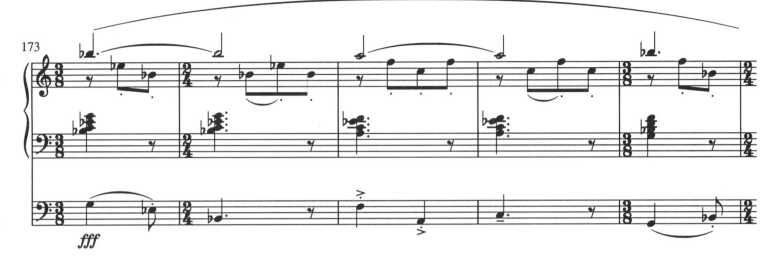

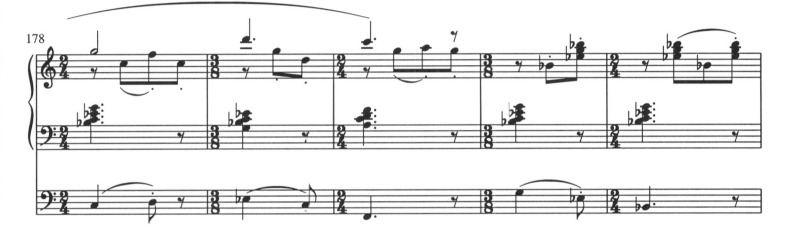

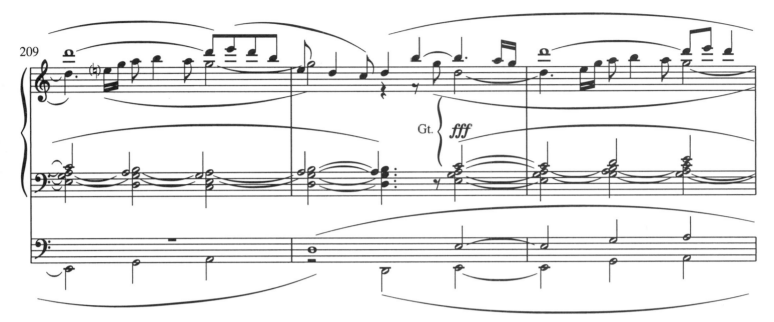

209

Gt. *fff*

212

**Quick and vibrant** (♩ = ca. 152)

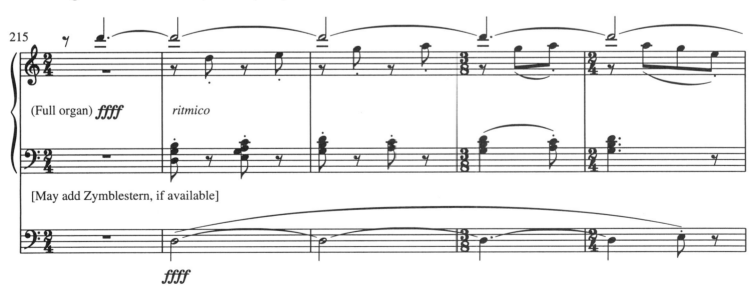

215

(Full organ) *ffff*  *ritmico*

[May add Zymblestern, if available]

*ffff*

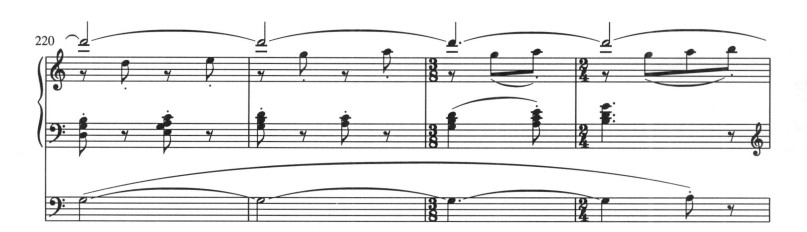

**(No slowing)**

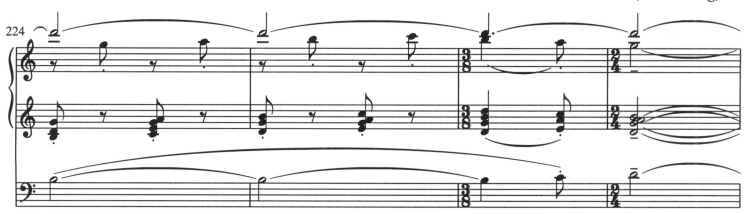

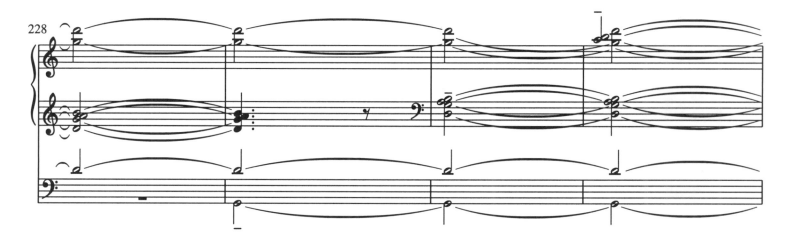

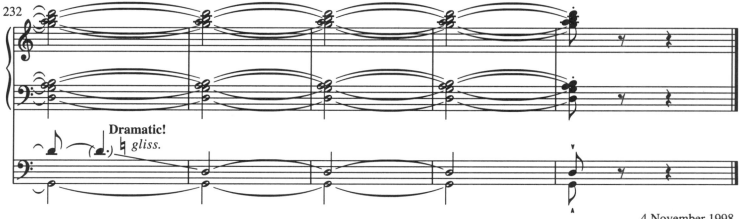

4 November 1998
Winston-Salem, NC